DK **READERS**

BEGINNING TO READ ALONE
2

I Want to Be a Gymnast

Written by Kate Simkins

Hannah and her friend Jessica
dream of being gymnasts one day.
They both go to a gymnastics club
twice a week and
they love it there.

Last week, the girls arrived
at the club after school.
They put on their leotards
in the changing rooms.

Then they ran
around the gym
to warm up.
"I hope I can
have a go on
the beam today,"
said Hannah
to her friend.

The other girls soon arrived and joined in the running.
Everyone started jumping and hopping as well.

These exercises warmed them up so that they wouldn't injure themselves in the gym.

"Good!" said Sarah, their coach. "You should be nice and warm by now!"

Standing tall
Learning how to stand straight and tall helps the girls look more graceful as they do gymnastics.

Next the girls did exercises to
stretch different parts of the body.
Stretching makes it easier
to do gymnastics.

Tyra was really good at forward bends.
She could easily touch her toes!

Hannah stretched
her feet.
Strong feet are
important if you want
to be a gymnast.

Then the girls did box splits.
Their legs were stretched out wide
to the side.

"Keep your back straight and
your head up!" Sarah told them.

Tyra stretched one leg to the front
and the other behind.
This is called front splits.

"I tried lots of times before I could
do it," she smiled.

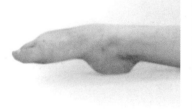

Pointed toes
Gymnasts should try to
point their toes.
It makes their legs look
longer and straighter.

The girls know they need
to be strong if they want
to be gymnasts.

Hannah climbed a rope
to strengthen her arms.

Look at the amazing shape
Tiggy made.
This shape is called the bridge and
is good for strengthening
your arms and legs.

Jessica loved
showing everyone
her forward rolls.

She tucked
her head and
knees in and
rolled like a ball.

Backward rolls are a bit harder.
Tiggy learnt how to do them by
using a sloping springboard
to help her.

"I want to do it again!" she said
after her first try.

"I'm worried
I'll fall over,"
said Tyra when
it was time to do
a headstand.

"Don't worry,
I'll help you,"
promised Molly.

Handstands
All gymnasts
need to be able
to do handstands.
Molly did
a handstand
without anyone
helping her.

Molly held Tyra
as she balanced
on her hands
and head, then
straightened
her legs.

"I did it!"
Tyra smiled.

"Can I go on
the beam yet?"
asked Hannah.

"Maybe later," Sarah replied.
"Try a cartwheel first."

The girls used
a bench to learn
how to do
a cartwheel.
They tried to
keep their legs
straight.

Then they had a go on the floor.

Jessica was really good.

She did four cartwheels in a row.

"It's funny being upside down!"
she laughed.

All the girls really enjoyed
jumping and leaping.
It was exciting to see how high
they could jump and
how far they could leap.

The trampoline
The trampoline is
really bouncy
and gives
you time to
make shapes
in the air.

Molly looked like she was flying as she leapt through the air.

Tiggy used the trampoline to do a pike jump with straight legs.

"Who wants to try the vault?"
asked Sarah.
"I do," cried Jessica, "but
it looks really high!"

Sarah showed her how to take off
from the springboard.

When she was ready,
Jessica sprang onto
the vault.

Straddle jump
A straddle jump is like leapfrog. Your legs are lifted high and wide above the vault.

She landed on the top and straddle jumped off again.

The girls were looking forward to
swinging on the asymmetric bars.
First they covered their hands
with chalk to stop them slipping.

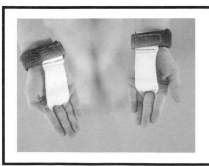

Handguards
Special covers are
worn on your hands
to stop them from
getting blisters.

Molly hung from the higher bar. She really enjoyed swinging backwards and forwards.

"Watch me stand on the bar!" said Tyra as Katie helped her balance.

"Hurrah! It's the beam," cried Hannah.

Hannah showed what she could do on the beam.

She balanced on one leg and pointed her toes.

The beam
The beam is only 10 centimetres (4 inches) wide. Top gymnasts can even do jumps on the beam.

Jessica, Tiggy and Tyra walked
along the beam.
It was hard not to wobble!

The lesson was over and
the girls talked about what
they had learnt.

Well done!
After a few months of lessons,
all the girls did well enough
to get their Gym
Skills Certificates.

Although the girls were quite tired,
they still had enough energy
to jump in the foam pit!

Hannah and Jessica love going to the gymnastics club.

They have made lots of new friends. If they work really hard, they will get better and better.

"I hope to be a champion gymnast one day," said Hannah.

"Perhaps we will even take part in the Olympic Games!" added Jessica.

But the most important thing is that they are having lots of fun!

Gymnastics Facts

Both female and male gymnasts take part in competitions.
The biggest competition is the Olympic Games.

One of the most famous gymnasts was
Nadia Comaneci.
She was the first gymnast to score a maximum ten points at the Olympics.

The vault is also called the vaulting horse.
It was first used by Roman soldiers to practise getting on their horses.

The asymmetric bars are two bars.
One is about 1.5 metres (5 feet) high.
The other is about 2.3 metres (7½ feet) high.